Original title:
A Succulent Affair

Copyright © 2025 Creative Arts Management OÜ
All rights reserved.

Author: Cameron Blair
ISBN HARDBACK: 978-1-80581-759-8
ISBN PAPERBACK: 978-1-80581-286-9
ISBN EBOOK: 978-1-80581-759-8

Flourishing Fantasies Under the Stars

In a garden bright, plants sway and dance,
With tipsy tomatoes, taking a chance.
Cucumbers giggle, oh what a sight,
Carrots in tutus, twirling at night.

A cabbage whispers, 'Let's throw a ball!'
While peppers strut, feeling ten feet tall.
In the moonlight, they laugh and jive,
Salsa rhythm helps them thrive.

The herbs join in, all spicy and grand,
Basil and sage, a pungent band.
They shake their leaves, what a bold flair,
Caught in the moment, without a care.

But heads turn when a gnat steals the show,
Buzzing around, putting on a glow.
The party's wild, oh what a blast,
Don't mind the bugs, let's make it last!

Sips of Color in Desert Breezes

Cacti wear a stylish hat,
Their spines a prickly welcome mat.
With every sip from tiny cups,
The desert drinks from nature's ups.

A birdsong echoes, oh so sweet,
As lizards dance with tiny feet.
We toast to blooms that boldly jest,
In shades of nature's vibrant zest.

Symphonies of Green and Gold

In gardens full of giggles bright,
The sunflowers reach for dizzy heights.
They sway and twirl with leafy grace,
Tickling bees as they brush past space.

Succulents wear a grin so wide,
A prickly crew we can't divide.
They join the band of nature's cheer,
In funny rhythms we all hear.

The Playful Form of Flora

A cactus tried a silly dance,
With arms that move as if in trance.
The daisies giggle, oh so loud,
As nature forms its playful crowd.

In pots and patches, colors clash,
The blooms all giggle in a splash.
A succulent's bright, cheeky grin,
Makes watering cans break out in sin.

Daring Currents in a Drought

Watering holes, a thirsty plight,
Yet plants throw parties day and night.
They wear their drought like fancy wear,
And laugh at sunshine's ruthless glare.

With roots so deep, they tease the heat,
A sneaky sip, their own retreat.
In this dry dance, they thrive and thrive,
Making even drought feel alive.

Lush Crochets of Nature's Palette

In a garden so bright, what a sight!
With cactus in bloom, it's pure delight.
They sway and they twirl, in a floral dance,
Even prickly ones dream of romance.

With hues so bold, they take the stage,
A flower child's quirky, wild page.
Amongst the greens, a vibrant crowd,
It's the plant party, oh so loud!

Intimate Moments Under the Sun

Two succulents sit, side by side,
Under the sun, they try to confide.
With whispers of love, they bask and grin,
Plotting their escape from the watering bin.

A wrinkled leaf turns a rosy hue,
As flirtation blooms in the afternoon dew.
They giggle and beam, each poke a tease,
Who knew romance was found with such ease?

Roots of Romance in Arid Land

In lands so dry, love finds a way,
With roots entwined, they play all day.
A tumbleweed rolls, with envy in tow,
While prickly buddies steal the show.

They share with glee, a couple of laughs,
A yucca strums tunes for their sweet gaffs.
With every ooh and each playful sigh,
These drought-tolerant hearts reach for the sky.

The Chorus of Bountiful Flora

The flowers unite, a quirky tune,
With petals that dance, they flirt with the moon.
In laughter they burst, the blossoms all sing,
Joyful and happy, their colors take wing.

Zinnias joke with the astute marigold,
While tulips spin tales, both wild and bold.
Roses roll their eyes, in playful jest,
Who knew such blooms could be so blessed?

The Garden's Tender Secrets

In a leafy corner, secrets grow,
Whispers from cacti, so soft and low.
A squirrel made a home in a pot,
And stole all the beans—oh, what a plot!

With each prickly hug and leafy kiss,
The garden's antics, you can't dismiss.
Beneath the blooms, there's mischief and glee,
Just ask the worms—they'll agree with me!

Vivid Textures Beneath the Heat

Under the sun, the colors clash,
With every bloom, I hear the splash.
A beetle strutted on a rose's thigh,
In a bright suit, oh my, oh my!

The garden's a party, everyone knows,
An oriole's dance, while the sweet thyme grows.
Each petal's a dancer, each leaf a fan,
Bringing the heat like a summer plan!

When Green Meets the Golden Hour

As day fades into a warm embrace,
The garden shimmies, finding its pace.
Old gnomes chuckle beneath the trees,
While bees share gossip with rustling leaves.

Golden sunbeams, a playful tease,
Dance on the daisies, stir up the bees.
Amid the laughter, a piglet prances,
Chasing his dreams—and a few wild glances!

Thorns and Petals in Delight

A rose with a thorn told a tale so bright,
'I'm prickly but charming, won't give you a fright!'
She winked at a daisy, who giggled with glee,
'Being bold is the key; just ask any bee!'

In a dance of colors, oh what a sight,
Thorns and petals twirling into the night.
With laughter and roots, both big and small,
The garden's a ball, come one, come all!

Nature's Sweet Confessions

In the garden, I found a pear,
Whispering secrets, a fruity affair.
It giggled with laughter, quite bold,
Telling tales of apples and mold.

A tomato blushed, round and red,
Wishing it could just leap from its bed.
With a wink, it dropped some seeds,
Promising growth, fulfilling needs.

The basil danced, a dazzling sight,
Twisting and turning, full of delight.
Chasing the thyme, oh what a chase,
In this green world, there's always space.

Yet the rhubarb sits, sulking there,
Grumbling softly, in deep despair.
"Why can't I be the star of the show?"
But even grumps grow when it's their row.

A Garden Awash with Emotions

Among the petals, a daisy cried,
Yearning for love, oh, how it sighed!
A bumblebee passed, buzzing with cheer,
And whispered, "Don't worry, I'll be near."

The carrots chuckled, sticking together,
While the lettuce got swayed by the weather.
"Let's dress up in soil and play in the rain,"
Every root laughed, causing a gain.

A sunflower tried to strike a pose,
But tripped on its leaves and fell on its nose.
With the crew laughing, it stood with pride,
"Next time, I'll land on the brighter side!"

The radishes blushed, red as a flame,
While the beets found the whole thing a game.
In this quirky patch, where nothing's too grim,
Every sprout knows life's just a whim.

Seductive Shades in the Evening Glow

Beet greens sway in a sultry beat,
Under the stars, they shimmy and greet.
With garlic smirking, and mint in a spin,
Whispers of flavor, where fun begins.

A radish winked, so crisp and so spry,
Challenging the peppers, "Let's give it a try!"
They lit up the night with colors so bright,
In this garden party, everything felt right.

Zucchini flaunted its curves in the light,
While herbs plotted mischief, a zany delight.
"Let's toss in a salad and dance 'round the bowl,
Eat up the laughter and savor the soul!"

Beneath the moon's glow, veggies rejoice,
Each crunch and each chew gives the night a voice.
In their own way, they're all quite the charm,
Each bite is a story, a flavorful balm.

The Gentle Sigh of a Cactus Rose

A cactus cracked a joke with a grin,
Nudging the roses, inviting a spin.
"Don't mind my prickles, I'm friendly, I swear!
It's just a spiky way of showing I care."

The daisies giggled, petals all askew,
"Are you sure you're tough? We could use a few!"
A bloom overhead piped in with flair,
"With spiky humor, life's never unfair!"

A tumbleweed rolled by, looking quite lost,
His path through the garden, at quite the cost.
"Can I crash this party, or am I too rough?"
But the gang just laughed, "Oh no, that's enough!"

So they danced in the moonlight, all colorful blooms,
Each one with a punchline, avoiding the glooms.
Who knew that a garden could serve up such fun?
With laughter and love under bright shining sun.

Green Dreams in the Peachy Dawn

In the garden, greens collide,
Tomatoes blush, the peppers slide.
Lettuce winks beneath the sun,
With carrots plotting playful fun.

Broccoli wears a crown of glee,
While zucchini dreams of being free.
Dancing leaves in morning's light,
Chasing bugs in sheer delight.

The herbs gossip, oh what a scene!
Basil's gossip, oregano's queen.
Mint teases thyme with a swift sway,
In this kitchen party, hip hooray!

But don't forget the salad bowl,
A veggie toss is good for the soul.
With all their quirks on display,
They laugh and play, come what may!

Silent Cravings Among Leafy Shadows

In shady corners, lettuce sighs,
Cucumbers dreaming of sunny skies.
Beetroot blushes, a deep maroon,
While spinach reveals its leafy tune.

Avocado whispers to the sprout,
'We'll find the perfect dish, no doubt.'
On this quiet, leafy dance floor,
They scheme of flavors to explore.

Carrots chuckle, their tops a-hair,
'Who knew we'd have such flair to share?'
With dips and dressings, a joyous spread,
A meal from thoughts that danced in head.

Peas pop out with a playful cheer,
Sprouting jokes that all can hear.
Together in laughter, veggies sway,
In this leafy lounge where friends play!

Flourishing in the Echoes of Earth

In the soil, a secret's kept,
As roots around their secrets crept.
Radishes giggle and onions pout,
What is this mess that sprouted out?

Garlic's whispers fill the ground,
'This underground's quite profound.'
With laughter echoing, plants unite,
In earthy joy, they find delight.

The blooms around, what a grand affair,
Petals swirl without a care.
Nectar sippers join the fun,
Buzzing happily, one by one.

Together they share the sunlit gleam,
A garden tale, a shared dream.
With playful spirits, they proclaim,
In living colors, they'll stake their claim!

A Tapestry of Flora and Desire

Lily pads float with lazy grace,
Sunflowers bask, a golden face.
Petunias gossip, stunning in bloom,
While bees insist they need more room.

Oh, watch the daisies flaunt their style,
Competing quietly all the while.
With petals bright and stems so bold,
In this garden, tales are told.

Cacti stand with prickly charm,
Laughing at the grass's alarm.
Each thorn a joke, each bloom a jest,
They claim their spot, they feel the best.

In a vibrant patch of sweet delight,
Flora dances, oh what a sight!
In this medley, filled with desire,
The laughter grows, the sparks inspire!

Nectar Kisses on the Sunlit Skin

A dripping fruit, oh what a tease,
So sweet it makes the buzzing bees.
We giggle as we take a bite,
Juicy moments, pure delight.

The sunbeam dances on our plate,
With every lick, no time to wait.
Sticky fingers, laughter flows,
In this sweet game, anything goes.

Beneath the shade, we share a drink,
A muddled mix that makes us wink.
With every sip, our worries fade,
A humorous toast, a sunny parade.

From blushing berries to mango's kiss,
Each fruity moment, we can't dismiss.
In this raucous feast, we find our bliss,
With laughter's echo, there's nothing amiss.

Opulent Succulence in Every Leaf

Oh leafy greens, you dress so fine,
With vinaigrette, a taste divine.
A crispy crunch that makes us smile,
A salad party, let's stay awhile.

Tomatoes pop like little jewels,
With every bite, we break the rules.
We twirl our forks, we spin around,
In this garden, joy is found.

When lettuce winks and peppers prance,
We can't resist the silly dance.
Each veggie glows with vibrant cheer,
Making healthy fun, that's our frontier.

So come and toss, don't hold back!
We'll make a mess, that's our knack.
In every leaf, a world so bright,
In laughter's warmth, we find our light.

Warm Hues of Passionate Flora

In the garden, colors clash,
With petals bright, oh what a stash!
Roses giggle, tulips twirl,
In floral fun, let laughter swirl.

Dandelions puff with joyful pride,
As bees approach, they laugh and hide.
With every blossom, jokes unfold,
A garden's tale, a joy to behold.

Sunflowers stand, tall and grand,
Waving arms like a playful band.
In this riot of color, wild and free,
Nature's humor, a sight to see.

With petals soft and stems so strong,
We dance along the garden song.
Forever bright, in hues we trust,
In laughing blooms, we find our lust.

The Art of Savoring Life

With every bite, we take our time,
Exploring flavors, like a rhyme.
A dash of spice, a pinch of glee,
Eating life, as fun can be.

We gather 'round, a feast in sight,
With silly hats, what a delight!
Forks in hand, we stack the plates,
In laughter's warmth, we celebrate.

Desserts arrive with joyful flair,
Chocolate drips, no need to care.
We dig right in, with messy hands,
In this sweet chaos, friendship stands.

Life's buffet, a vibrant mix,
We savor all, from sips to fix.
In every bite, joy comes alive,
With laughter and love, we truly thrive.

Alchemy of Earth and Heart

In a pot, they dance and sway,
Green fingers taste the sunny day.
With a sip of water, they will cheer,
Growing stout, they'll drink the beer.

Cacti giggle in their spines,
While succulents toast with lime.
Rooted jokes in every leaf,
Their humor offers comic relief.

Hugging rocks and sand so tight,
They're partying till the night!
With a wink, they'll sprout a smile,
In the garden, laughter's style!

Blushing blooms in colors bright,
Playing tricks in morning light.
Funky shades and funny hats,
Who knew plants could be so brats?

Dreaming with Succulent Eyes

Underneath a leafy roof,
The dreams plant puns, oh what goof!
Shades of green, they build a plot,
In this garden, laughter's caught.

Loopy leaves and pearly dew,
Here's a secret, just for you!
They gossip about the snails,
Who tried to climb but left their trails.

Aloe quips, "I'm feeling bright,
But these pests don't treat me right!"
Echeveria rolls her eyes,
While sipping sunlight, oh so wise!

In the night, they dream of fun,
With moonlit jokes, their laughter spun.
Who knew greens could have such sass?
With every wink, they let time pass!

Serenade of the Sun-Kissed

Beaming rays on plump delight,
Succulents sing with all their might.
With potted joy, they belt a tune,
Underneath a glowing moon.

"Join us, friends!" the jade one calls,
"Life is best with dance and brawls!"
Cactus cracks a one-liner here,
"Just don't make me shed a tear!"

They sway with breezes, oh so spry,
Banter floats, the time flies by.
With laughter shared in every sprout,
They know what life's about!

So raise a glass to leafy life,
Avoiding all the garden strife.
In sun-kissed joy, they sing and play,
These cheeky greens are here to stay!

The Art of Green Affection

Plant love notes in earthen beds,
Scribbled secrets for their heads.
Clinging tightly, roots entwined,
These greens show love that's well-defined.

"Let's grow old," the robust sage,
"Together we'll hit every stage."
Jokes about water flow like wine,
These leafy hearts are simply divine!

In succulent life, there's no regret,
Each leaf a promise, never a fret.
The art of love beneath the sun,
Each sprout a tale of joy begun!

So cherish friends with greens so bright,
With quirky humor, day and night.
In this garden, we find our space,
Where laughter blooms, and smiles embrace!

Fragile Footprints on Sandy Shores

Tiny toes dance on grains of gold,
Each step a giggle, stories unfold.
Seagulls chuckle, peck at my snack,
While I trip on shells—no turning back.

Waves whisper secrets, teasing my feet,
A soggy sandal? Oh, that's quite the feat!
Sandcastle dreams, they crumble and fall,
Laughter erupts, it's the best of all!

The sun's in my eyes, my hat's on the line,
I'm melting like chocolate, oh how divine!
Yet each salty breeze brings joy anew,
With footprints fading, I dance in the dew.

So here's to the beach, where mishaps abound,
In fragile footprints, pure happiness found.
With friends all around, life's a goofy delight,
Let's frolic in sand till the moon shines bright.

Harmony in the Garden of Thorns

In a garden where roses and cacti embrace,
I trip over petals in this floral race.
Bees buzz with laughter, they swarm like a choir,
While I dodge a thorn, my slip, oh, what a dire!

We dance through the daisies, a waltz so absurd,
The daisies are laughing; I'm feeling quite stirred.
Tangled in vines, I giggle and twirl,
Nature's odd rhythm, a quirky swirl!

The veggies are grinning, it's quite the scene,
Carrots are winking, the fun gets obscene!
Radishes snicker, tomatoes just roll,
In this tangled garden, we're all on a roll!

So let's toast with petals, raise a glass to the fun,
In harmony, we play till the day is all done.
A garden of laughter, where joy truly soars,
Among thorns and flowers, let's dance and explore!

The Allure of Amber Dew

Morning's bright sparkle, the dew hangs with glee,
Like little gems glistening, daring at me.
I sip on my coffee—wait, this tastes strange!
The ants threw a party, oh how they exchange!

Amber droplets lure me, with promises sweet,
But sticky fingers make for a slippery treat.
A dance with the bugs? Oh, do I dare go!
Try not to giggle, just don't make it a show!

The grass whispers secrets, tickling my toes,
While I'm prancing about, that's just how it goes.
Waltzing with blossoms, I dip and I sway,
But tripped over mud—oh heavens, hooray!

So here's to the dew and the morning delight,
With laughter and stumbles, we'll leap into the light.
The allure of the amber, so charming and true,
In this merry adventure, let's dance in the dew!

Tangy Echoes of Longing

In a kitchen of chaos, spices arise,
A tangy affair fills the air with surprise.
Lemons are giggling as they roll off the shelf,
While I juggle a bowl—look out for myself!

Saucy shenanigans, splatters galore,
The pasta's a conga; I can't help but roar.
As onions are sizzling, the laughter erupts,
I taste what I chopped—oops, who needs to cook?

Seasons are flirting, a flavor parade,
With each zesty zing, a grand escapade.
My taste buds are dancing, oh what a thrill,
Cooking's a comedy, a joy, what a skill!

So here's to the tang, the zest on the plate,
In echoes of laughter, we celebrate fate.
With each sizzle and pop, we savor the fun,
In this vibrant kitchen, joy's just begun!

Juicy Conversations Among the Foliage

In the garden where cacti dance,
Sassy succulents steal a glance.
Chatter blooms with each bright sprout,
Whispers sweet, a playful shout.

The aloe jokes with the jade plant,
Their banter grows, it's quite the chant.
"Let's have a party, no need for dew,
Just a little sunshine, a drink or two!"

Under the sun, they frolic and sway,
Sharing secrets, come what may.
"Stop hogging the sunlight!" one shrieks in glee,
"Don't be so prickly, just let it be!"

With laughter ringing through the heat,
Cactus flowers stomp their feet.
In this grand patch of green delight,
Every leaf is a chatterbox, oh what a sight!

Blooming Hearts in the Dry Season

In desert heat, a sun-kissed bloom,
Hearts are bright, dispelling gloom.
Cacti blush with little flair,
Whispers sweet, love's in the air.

"Why do you poke?" the bloom doth sigh,
"Can't help it, dear, I'm a spiky guy!"
Yet each touch ignites a spark,
Two hearts thump beneath the dark.

A yucca's giggles, so full of spice,
"Let's dance beneath the stars tonight!"
The moonlit romance, a grand charade,
In this dry land, love's never afraid.

So let the saguaro sway and twist,
In blooming hearts, they can't resist.
A prickly pair, now hand in hand,
In this sunburnt but tender land!

The Allure of Moisture and Light

Sunshine glints on leaves so bright,
While roots wiggle for moisture, it's a delight.
"Can we go clubbing?" a fern does plea,
"Only if it's close to the potting tree!"

Each droplet's like a splash of fun,
Dewy mornings, oh how they run!
"Too much sun and I might dry out,
But with the right light, I'll dance about!"

In puddles gleefully they splash,
Giggling softly with a seaweed crash.
"Moisture, dear friend, is the key to glow,
So let's gather 'round; we're ready to show!"

So let the moisture flow, cascade,
In laughter, joy, the plan is laid.
With light as their stage, they twirl and ignite,
A beautiful dance, oh what a sight!

Incandescent Hues of Earthly Love

In raucous hues, the blossoms peek,
A riot of colors, unique and cheeky.
"Red for passion, but maybe some green,
Let's mix it up; be bold and keen!"

Petals twinkle under the sky,
"Who knew plants could be so spry?"
Dancing under sunlit rays,
Painting the world in radiant ways.

"Let's throw a rave, with vines as our lights!
Bring all the pots; we'll party through nights!"
With laughter erupting, they twirl and tangle,
In the garden's embrace, they joyfully wrangle.

So here's to the colors that lighten the day,
Each hue a laughter, in its own little way.
In incandescent love, they all find their groove,
For life's a grand dance, when you've got the right moves!

A Love Letter to Green Delights

Oh, green beauties on my plate,
You fill my heart and elevate.
With every crunch, my spirit soars,
Who knew veggies could open doors?

Your colors dance, a weird parade,
Each bite's a joke, a joyful trade.
With laughter sweet in every meal,
It's a romance I can feel!

From leafy greens to fruits that tease,
You make my taste buds feel at ease.
This love affair with vibrant hues,
Brings silly smiles, no time to lose!

So here's my heartfelt, joyful cheer,
To all the greens that bring good cheer.
I'll munch you down with pure delight,
Let's savor snacks, both day and night!

Drifting Through a Jungle of Colors

In a jungle where flavors blend,
Bold and bright, they never end.
I swing from fruit to leafy greens,
Chasing tastes like wild, unseen!

Tropical hues make crazy pairs,
With giggles lost in food affairs.
Pineapples wink, and mangoes grin,
It's a feast where fun begins!

I trip on veggies, awkward dance,
Tumbling down this salad chance.
Veggies in a tango, wild and proud,
Cheering loudly, oh so loud!

Through this jungle, I shall roam,
With tasty bites that feel like home.
Each silly crunch, a playful jest,
This vibrant feast is simply the best!

Silken Petals and Heat-Heavy Days

On soft petals, the sun does tease,
Melting moments down with ease.
With laughter bubbling, sweet and slick,
Every sticky bite's a funny trick!

Heat heavy days, they come and go,
I seek the chill of fruity flow.
In shades of pink and radiant gold,
Bite-sized mischief, stories told!

I drip and drop in a fruity whirl,
As sticky bits make my heart twirl.
A slushy giggle, a gooey embrace,
In this sweet chaos, I find my place!

With silken treats, I swirl and sway,
Laughing through the heat of the day.
A blissful mess, oh what a sight,
In this flavor fest, I feel so right!

Tangy Moments Caught in Time

In tangy bites, I find my groove,
Combining zesty, crazy moves.
Each splash of flavor brings a grin,
Who knew sour could feel like sin?

With zest explosions, laughter blends,
Tickling senses, the fun transcends.
Lemon and lime, a cheeky mix,
Citrus jokes, the best quick fix!

Caught in a whirl of flavors bold,
These tangy moments never get old.
I sip and munch, a joyful spree,
Turning sour into glee!

Each little bite, a punchline true,
Tickles the palate, just for you.
Let's celebrate this silly feast,
With every tang, my joy increased!

The Shades of Abundant Affection

In pots so round, they bounce and sway,
Their leaves in colors bright and gay.
We water them with laughter's kiss,
A playful bond we can't dismiss.

Each spiky friend, a quirky mate,
In sunlit spots, they love to play.
They cheer us up when days are rough,
Their tales of growth, oh, aren't they tough?

We share our snacks, we speak in glee,
They nod along, quite cheerfully.
A cactus joke or two we'll tell,
In this small green paradise, we dwell.

So here's to plants with silly quirks,
In their lush world, we are the perks.
With roots entwined, our giggles grow,
In shades of love, the joy will flow.

Unwritten Sonnets Among the Succulents

The aloe's sharp, but so refined,
With stories wild and winks aligned.
A poem waits, on leaves it's scrawled,
In laughter's tune, we are enthralled.

The jade plant smiles, a beacon bright,
In moonlit nights, it twinkles light.
We scribble dreams on sandy ground,
As giggles burst, and love is found.

A rolling stone, a pebble's song,
We dance about where we belong.
Two tall agaves play a game,
Their tussling leaves, a lively claim.

With puns and quirks, a tale we weave,
In every pot, our hearts believe.
As sapphires grow and petals jive,
In this lush plot, we thrive alive.

Petals of Exuberance and Charm

With petals soft and faces wide,
Each bloom's a joke that we can't hide.
They crack us up with every sway,
In colors bold, they dance and play.

A wedding feast for bees and buds,
We chuckle loud, make merry thuds.
In every pot, a party's planned,
With sunlight bright, it's simply grand.

Chubby cheeks of leafy greens,
In shady spots, they wear their sheens.
We toast with tea, watch shadows dance,
In the succulent world, we take a chance.

So raise a glass to nature's glee,
With every leaf, we sing with glee.
In laughter's light, our hearts will warm,
In petal soft, we'll weather the storm.

Juicy Whispers in the Heat

In summer's grip, we laugh and sigh,
The plants gossip as we walk by.
With every sip, we share a tale,
In cactus lounges, we'll prevail.

A dandelion in full bloom,
Dreams take flight in fragrant room.
With juicy quirks and sunny rays,
We spend our time in playful ways.

The prickly pear throws shade with flair,
Its jokey thorns create a scare.
We giggle as the sun goes down,
In leafy comforts, we won't frown.

So here's to summers packed with fun,
In nature's arms, we've just begun.
With whispers sweet, the critters cheer,
In juicy worlds, we banish fear.

Thorns Cradle Sweetness

In a patch of spikes and light,
I found a love that felt just right.
Her laughter danced like petals fair,
Yet watch your step, beware the snare.

We twirled around, a prickly waltz,
With every twist, we felt the pulse.
She giggles sweet, then pokes my arm,
This thorny love, it has a charm!

I brought her sweets and she brought zest,
Our chemistry, a cactus fest.
Hearts wrapped tight in prickly hugs,
This cannot be, just call it 'thugs.'

So here we are, a jolly pair,
In love, you see, with added flair.
Life's a slice of crunchy pie,
With every thorn, we laugh and sigh!

Romance in the Cactus Garden

Among the spines, we stroll and sway,
Each tiny bloom, a bold display.
She whispers secrets to the breeze,
While rubbing cactus, if you please!

A dance of stubbed toes on soft ground,
In this weird world, love's unbound.
With every scrape that makes me howl,
We forge our path, both fun and foul!

The sun sets down, our shadows blend,
In nature's arms, we make amends.
We toast with roots and flower wine,
Who knew this chaos could be divine?!

So grab your hat and take a chance,
In this wild place, we'll cha-cha dance.
With laughter loud, we shake the gloom,
And call this random love our bloom!

Velvety Sips of Paradise

We sip on nectar, soft and sweet,
In a garden where oddities meet.
With giggles bright, our glasses clink,
This life of thorns makes me rethink!

Every drop, a punchline plays,
While we bask in the sun's warm rays.
Oh, look at that, a cactus dive,
A splash of joy, we feel alive!

She dribbles juice down her chin,
And suddenly, I can't help but grin.
Her laughter echoes in the air,
These quirky moments, nothing compares!

So let's revel in this zany spree,
In every prick, there's glee, you see.
With velvety sips, we seal the deal,
This funny love, it's just surreal!

The Tangle of Vines and Dreams

Amidst the vines, we twist and twirl,
In a dreamscape where jokes unfurl.
Each tendril wraps, a playful tie,
In this wild web, we dare to fly!

Her puns fly high like blooms in spring,
While I pretend to be a king.
Yet royalty is full of pricks,
In this jungle, we trade our tricks!

We sprawl 'neath stars, our laughter sings,
The tangled knots of love it brings.
With every giggle, we steal the night,
Vines of mischief, what a sight!

So here we spin, a dizzy dance,
In this delightful, viney romance.
With tangled hearts, we face the quake,
In laughter's grip, no room for ache!

Whispers of Juicy Summer

In the garden, fruits giggle bright,
Melons in shorts, a comical sight.
Cucumbers prance, all green and spry,
While tomatoes blush, oh my, oh my!

Peppers tell tales, their heat a jest,
Radishes, shy, wear greens like a vest.
Lemonade waits, a chilled summer treat,
While all of us dance, and stomp our feet!

Sentinels of the Drought

Cactus guards the parched, lonely land,
Pointy and proud, like an outstretched hand.
With a hat made of sun and boots full of sand,
He winks at the clouds, they just never planned.

Daisies essay a break in the heat,
Giggling buds, bringing laughter and sweet.
Cracking up soil, they try to take flight,
With dreams of a shower on this dry night!

Lush Embrace in Desert's Heart

Within the dunes, a party's afoot,
Succulents swaying, all in their roots.
They toss out invites in soft, warm air,
A dance with the lizards, without a care!

Jade leaves shimmy, like they own the floor,
While agave giggles, but craves something more.
The moon takes a sip from the nearby creek,
As night creeps in, the succulents speak!

Nectar Drops at Dusk

Dew drops gather, a sweet little tease,
As petals uncurl to catch evening's breeze.
Bees swarm around, a buzzing delight,
Trading jokes with the stars in twilight.

Hummingbirds flirt, they dip and they dive,
With nectar so rich, they plan to arrive.
In this garden of giggles, old secrets are spun,
As dusk settles softly, the laughter's begun!

Forbidden Fruits Beneath the Stars

Under a moonlit tree, they quarreled,
With apples in hand, quite overwhelmed.
"Just take a bite, it's not that bad!"
"Last time, I left feeling quite mad!"

Peaches whispered secrets, soft and sly,
While cherries giggled, "Oh, my, oh my!"
The nectar sweet, a sticky affair,
Fruit-fueled romances hanging in air.

Avocado dreams, so smooth and bright,
Kissed by salsa, a tantalizing bite.
"Let's pickle our love!" they cried in glee,
"Just don't forget, you'll always need me!"

In the garden of love, they swayed and spun,
It's all fun and games until they're done.
Beneath the stars, with laughter they feast,
Their endless desires, a humorous beast.

Mirage of Love Blossoms

In a desert of dreams, the cacti sway,
With prickly charm in a playful way.
"Is love just skin deep?" they quizzed with a grin,
"Or is it like watering a cactus within?"

A daisy popped up, feeling quite bold,
"Watch me bloom! My secrets unfold!"
But oh, that sunflower, with head turned away,
"Keep your petals, I'm here to play!"

Pineapple wisdom, a crown on top,
Declared, "Life's juicy, don't ever stop!"
With laughter and jests, they twisted and turned,
Under shimmering stars, their passions burned.

While roses rolled over with petal jubilee,
They danced through the night, wild and free.
With every poke and playful tease,
Love's a mirage, but who's keeping the fees?

The Secret Life of Leafy Hearts

In a jungle of thoughts, they planted their love,
With leafy affection and stars up above.
"Are we green enough?" said the fern with a sigh,
While the ivy just chuckled, "Oh, let's give it a try!"

The daisies giggled, swaying with glee,
"Let's play hide and seek behind the big tree!"
But the bark rolled its eyes with a creaky old laugh,
"Who knew leafy hearts could cause such a rift?"

Celery stalks in a secretive plot,
Dreamed of romance, but forgot what they've got.
With lettuce in hand, they raised a toast,
"To leafy love, we adore the most!"

As petals chattered, the night grew bright,
In the secretive garden, they danced with delight.
Friends in the foliage, their hearts made of green,
In nature's embrace, love's antics unseen.

Evocative Shadows in Bloom

In twilight's glow, shadows danced anew,
With daisies in hand, love's playful view.
"Shall we bloom where we're planted?" they chimed,
While tulips sighed gently, feeling unprimed.

"Lilacs are lovely!" shouted a rose,
"Yet thorns are all I ever chose!"
So under the stars, they spun and twirled,
In colorful chaos, their antics unfurled.

"Let's sprinkle some pollen, make it a fling!"
"Who needs a lover when you've got spring?"
The shadows kept whispering secrets that night,
With blooms overlapping, oh what a sight!

While giggles erupted from each little bud,
They basked in their charm, with hearts made of mud.
In a patchwork of petals, they laughed till the end,
In a garden of chaos, love is the trend.

Layers of Love in Elysian Earth

In gardens neat, our secrets hide,
Among the greens our giggles slide.
A cactus winks, a rose's grin,
With thorny jokes, we laugh and spin.

The soil's rich tales of joy and jest,
Where roots entwine, we're truly blessed.
A leaf falls down, but laughter's up,
In nature's bowl, we share our cup.

Each sprout a laugh, each bud a spark,
In this embrace, we leave our mark.
With watering cans, we joke around,
And in this mess, true love is found.

So let us dance through vine and thorn,
In every bloom, our hearts are worn.
We plant our dreams, we tend with care,
In layers thick, we share our flair.

Petal Kisses under Blue Skies.

Petals flutter like playful waves,
Under blue skies where laughter braves.
Each flower blushes, giving cheer,
While bees buzz by with peanut butter sneer.

Sipping nectar, sweet delight,
We steal a kiss, oh what a sight!
With honeyed words, we charm and tease,
In bloom's embrace, we find our ease.

A tulip's wink, a daffodil's grin,
In this bouquet, where love begins.
With swirling scents that tickle our nose,
We dance amidst a fragrant prose.

So grab a petal, let's make a wish,
In this garden, we won't miss.
Under sunny skies, our hearts take flight,
With every kiss, it feels just right.

Whispers of the Desert Bloom

In sandy dunes, we weave our laughs,
Among the cacti, we take our baths.
Beneath the sun, our shenanigans grow,
With prickly humor, we steal the show.

A succulent wink, a spiky embrace,
In this dry land, we find our place.
With every bloom, a quirky tale,
We giggle loud as the coyotes wail.

Oh, watch the lizards dance and tease,
As we share stories like the desert breeze.
With laughter bright as the midday sun,
In blooming chaos, we have our fun.

So let the sandstorms swirl around,
In this wild bloom, we are spellbound.
With whispers soft and smiles wide,
In desert love, we twist and glide.

Lush Embraces in Sunlit Corners

In sunlit nooks, our laughter blooms,
Among the greens, we banish glooms.
A friendly leaf waves to say hello,
While shady branches put on a show.

With vines that twist like love's embrace,
In streaks of light, we find our space.
A flower giggles, a petal jumps,
As we leap over the gardening lumps.

The sun is bright, but oh, so hot,
We sip our drinks in the small shade spot.
With joyous cheers and nature's zest,
In this lush land, we feel so blessed.

So gather round, bring friends and cheer,
In every corner, love draws near.
With hearty laughs, we own the day,
In sunny gardens, we find our way.

Prickly Encounters at Twilight

Beneath the stars, cacti sway,
A dance of spines, in their own way.
Two lovers meet, with hearts aligned,
But watch your step, or you'll be blind.

A giggle shared through sheer surprise,
As prickles poke, then laughter flies.
With every poke, their spirits soar,
Injured hearts, but craving more.

Moonlit whispers, a playful tease,
'Though you're prickly, I find you a breeze.'
They trip and tumble, no harm done,
In this strange game, they're the best of fun.

So raise a glass to those who dare,
To love amidst the prickly flair.
Twilight's charm and nature's kiss,
In every jab, there's blissful bliss.

Blushing Petals in Arid Lands

In dusty dunes, where laughter grows,
Petals blush in vibrant rows.
A flower's wink, a clever scheme,
Nature's prank on love's sweet dream.

Two blooms chat with silly grace,
Flaunting hues in this dry place.
Spritz of water, and off they go,
In a tumble, they steal the show.

Sunburned blush turns to a cheer,
Between the blooms, there's naught to fear.
Wrapped in petals, a silly sight,
Their love is fragrant, pure delight.

So in the heat, they find some fun,
Under the sun, they run and run.
With every giggle, hearts expand,
In arid lands, life's grand plan.

Savoring the Essence of Green

In gardens lush, where things grow wild,
A playful frog leaps, oh so styled.
He croaks a tune, invites a few,
To join his jamboree in the dew.

Amidst the greens, a banquet's laid,
Sap and zest in a dapper parade.
With every crunch, the laughter spikes,
Gastronomic joy, oh what delights!

Veggies roll in a salsa dance,
Courgettes boast of their fine romance.
With every swig of grassy drink,
They giggle, wiggle, and start to blink.

So gather round, don't make a scene,
In this lush world, life's fit to glean.
Savor the fun, in leafy schemes,
Essence of green fuels our dreams.

Seduction in the Sunlit Oasis

In the bright glow of a sandy bay,
A coconut smiles in a cheeky way.
With straws that sip and fruits that tease,
The sunlit charms bring lovers to their knees.

A sun-kissed breeze stirs up the fun,
Bikini blooms, oh what a run!
With every splash in the salt-sweet sea,
Their hearts entwine, wild and free.

Cacti sip from piña coladas,
Flirty flares, and cheeky baladas.
In this oasis, the days are long,
With laughter strumming a silly song.

So roll with us in this bright scene,
Where every glance is pure and keen.
In the sun's arms, love finds a way,
With a cheeky grin, we're here to stay.

Dainty Echoes Amidst Thorny Gardens

In gardens where laughter grows,
A cactus wears a flower's pose.
With prickles that dance in the breeze,
It teases bees, "Come here, if you please!"

But watch your step on velvet trails,
For toes can tangle in green scales.
The roses giggle, their petals bright,
While the thorns conspire to start a fight!

Even succulents join in the game,
Chatting softly, with no hint of fame.
With pots so cute, they're quite a sight,
A succulent meeting, oh what delight!

Yet humor hides in petals bright,
As nature's pranksters ignite the night.
With a wink, they plot and then they twist,
In this thorny garden, you can't resist!

The Enchantment of Arid Blossoms

In droughts where joy is hard to find,
A chubby plant catches the mind.
With plumpness that bursts, it's quite a feat,
It giggles and jiggly sways to the beat.

Oh, desert blooms with colors so bold,
They flirt with the sun, their stories told.
Each petal a wink, a tongue-in-cheek cheer,
While lizards watch from cozy spheres.

They throw a party when nights get cool,
Under the stars, they dance like fools.
While laughter bubbles in every pot,
Arid blossoms steal the show — on the dot!

But watch out for that prickly shrub,
It tries to join but becomes the grub.
With humor mixed in this dry delight,
Arid blooms make the evening bright!

Memoirs Caught in Thorns

Oh, the tales that spiky folks can tell,
In memoirs where prickly treasures dwell.
With every jab a story unfolds,
Of bees in disguise and daring bolds.

In corners where the sunlight skips,
Thorns have secret, scandalous trips.
They whisper of evenings, mischief at dawn,
When everyone's curious to know who's gone!

The tales of the night-shade thorns abound,
Like gossiping friends, they gather round.
With laughter and squabbles in every brush,
These memoirs of gardens are quite the hush!

So raise a glass to the thorny crew,
For memories made beneath the dew.
In this prickly abode, friendships thrive,
With thorny comfort, we all come alive!

Brewed Moments Between the Greens

In a pot of wonder, giggles sprout,
Leaves sip tea while taking a route.
Caught brewing tales in the leafy nook,
Where gossip stirs in every cook.

Succulent sips from muddy cups,
In every drink, the laughter erupts.
With whispers of thorns and rose-tinted tales,
Fluffy snacks are served, and humor prevails.

Oh, the greens clink cups, with a splash!
"To prickly friends and a welcoming bash!"
With every sip, more secrets are shared,
Such brewed moments, no one prepared!

So here's to the joy in every sip,
Where friendships blossom on this trip.
In the pot of greens, with laughter abloom,
A garden of fun dispels every gloom!

Sun-Kissed Revelations in Deep Hues

In the garden where whispers bloom,
Gossipy vines unfold their room.
The cactus pricks with playful glee,
While daisies giggle, 'Come see me!'

Bees dance like they own the sun,
Chasing shadows, oh what fun!
With each petal, secrets shared,
In hues of joy, we all get paired.

The sun dips low, a golden cheer,
Hot tomatoes, we hold dear.
With ripe laughter and juicy bites,
We toast to days that feel so bright.

Oh, the soil's got a story too,
Of roots entangled, a funny crew.
We give a smile, a wink, a cheer,
As blossoms burst—what a nice sphere!

Hushed Mornings with Room for Love

Morning mist hugs the sleepy grass,
While robins chirp as if to sass.
A pot of mint begins to sway,
Whispering secrets of the day.

Tomatoes yawn, their green tops stretch,
In a clumsy dance, they try to fetch.
Tangled tendrils with tales so sly,
Our plants know love, oh me, oh my!

The coffee brews, a fragrant kiss,
In this quiet moment, pure bliss.
Figs and olives join the show,
In hushed warmth, our laughter flows.

Sunshine peeks through leaves above,
While the garden hums of sweet love.
With every sprout and every sigh,
We cultivate joy, way up high.

Under the Sorrows of a Watering Can

With a heavy heart, the can weeps slow,
Pouring woes on rows of slow-growing woe.
Yet daisies dance, their petals in cheer,
Competing with weeds—oh dear, oh dear!

Succulents giggle, 'We thrive on neglect,'
With their prickly charm, they offer respect.
While ferns flutter like they own the air,
Teasing our hopes, without a care.

Beneath the surface, roots intertwine,
Secrets tucked in soil, oh how divine!
With every splash from that heavy can,
A round of laughter improves the plan.

So, we water not just with tears,
But jokes and joy, dispelling our fears.
Life in the garden spins round and round,
In the dance of the plants, pure joy is found.

Melodies of Rooted Connections

Roots intertwine like gossiping friends,
As laughter sprouts where the blue jay bends.
With every sprout, new stories we weave,
In the whispers of soil, we dare to believe.

Hilarious tomfoolery on every leaf,
Nature's comedy, a moment of relief.
Barking at shadows, the squirrels do jest,
Amidst buzzing bees, we feel quite blessed.

In this symphony of green and gold,
Each petal grins, with stories untold.
Through leafy arches, we celebrate bliss,
Rooted connections, not one we'll miss.

So come, take a seat, for the show has begun,
With a chorus of laughter, we bask in the sun.
An orchestra of nature plays boldly and free,
In this garden of humor, there's room for you and me.

www.ingramcontent.com/pod-product-compliance
Lightning Source LLC
Chambersburg PA
CBHW072135070526
44585CB00016B/1684